INSECTS AS...

PRODUCERS

ANNETTE WHIPPLE

Rourke
Educational Media

rourkeeducationalmedia.com

*Scan for Related Titles
and Teacher Resources*

Before Reading:

Building Academic Vocabulary and Background Knowledge

Before reading a book, it is important to tap into what your child or students already know about the topic. This will help them develop their vocabulary, increase their reading comprehension, and make connections across the curriculum.

1. *Look at the cover of the book. What will this book be about?*
2. *What do you already know about the topic?*
3. *Let's study the Table of Contents. What will you learn about in the book's chapters?*
4. *What would you like to learn about this topic? Do you think you might learn about it from this book? Why or why not?*
5. *Use a reading journal to write about your knowledge of this topic. Record what you already know about the topic and what you hope to learn about the topic.*
6. *Read the book.*
7. *In your reading journal, record what you learned about the topic and your response to the book.*
8. *After reading the book complete the activities below.*

Content Area Vocabulary
Use glossary words in a sentence.

colony
domestic
glazes
metamorphosis
molt
regurgitates
salivary glands
secrete
synthetic
textiles

After Reading:

Comprehension and Extension Activity

After reading the book, work on the following questions with your child or students in order to check their level of reading comprehension and content mastery.

1. *How long does a silk moth live as an adult? (Summarize)*
2. *Why do sericulturists harvest the cocoons of the silk moth before they emerge into adults? (Infer)*
3. *What are some uses for shellac? (Asking questions)*
4. *Why does honey never spoil? (Text to self connection)*
5. *When cochineal insects drink the sap from the prickly pear what does this help them to produce? (Asking questions)*

Extension Activity

This book talks about carmine and the everyday products it is used in. Take a tour around your house and see how many things you can find that contain carmine. Start in the kitchen and read the ingredient labels on the food products in your home. Continue to look at other things such as cosmetic products and clothing. Make a list of all the things you find that contain carmine. Are you surprised at how many things you found?

Table of Contents

Seeing Red: The Cochineal Scale Insect

Food and **textiles** have been dyed for centuries. One particular red dye made from the cochineal scale insect has been used for thousands of years. This dye is called cochineal, or carmine, after the carminic acid the cochineal insect produces to ward off predators. Cochineal insects were the first to make a strong, vibrant red dye.

In southern Mexico and Peru, the cochineal's native home, carmine dye was used for medicine, food, cosmetics, art, and textiles. Spanish conquistadors took cochineal-dyed fabric to Europe in 1519. Soon, European merchants exported the cochineal-dyed cloth to the Middle East, India, Africa, and the Americas. Carmine use expanded and became part of the global trade.

Cochineals are now harvested mainly in Peru and the Canary Islands on plantations of prickly pear cacti, the bugs' preferred host.

All cochineal insects live on the prickly pear cactus. The small, silver, oval insects are about one-third the size of a ladybug. They cluster together to drink sap from the cactus pads. This diet enables them to produce the red pigment called carmine.

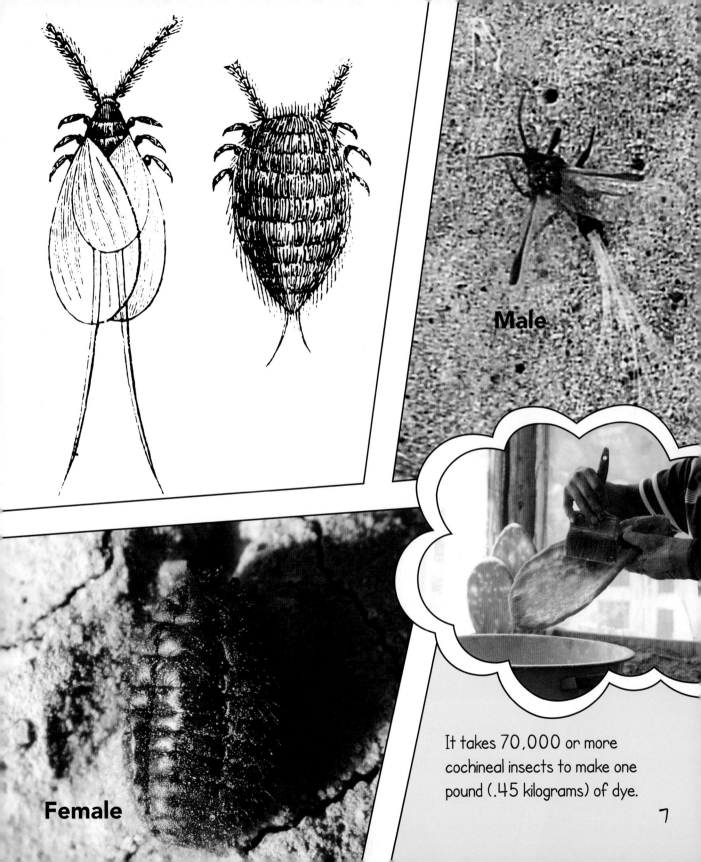

Male

Female

It takes 70,000 or more cochineal insects to make one pound (.45 kilograms) of dye.

7

After the insects are sun-dried and ground, they are dunked in an acidic alcohol solution to produce carminic acid, the pigment that eventually becomes carmine.

Harvesters collect live cochineal insects from the prickly pear cactus. Next, the insects are dried. The dead bodies are collected and ground into carmine powder used in dyes.

Carmine provides red coloring found in many foods and cosmetics. Packaged foods including candy, ice cream, yogurt, and beverages may include carmine as a coloring ingredient. Cosmetics such as blush, lipstick, and eyeshadow are often produced with carmine. Manufacturers often choose carmine because it produces strong red tones without artificial coloring.

LOOK FOR IT!

The United States Food and Drug Administration (FDA) requires carmine to be listed on food and cosmetic labels as "cochineal extract" or "carmine." Canada and some other countries call it "E120."

9

Sweet as Honey: Honeybee

Worker honeybees sting only for protection. They are the only bee that dies after stinging. Drone bees do not have a stinger.

People have used honey and other bee products since ancient times. Egyptians became the first beekeepers thousands of years ago. People still collect the honey and wax bees produce.

As social insects, bees work together in the hive to serve one purpose: to produce more honeybees for the benefit of the **colony**. A hive may contain as many as 50,000 bees. Even in large colonies, there is only one queen bee. Her job is to lay eggs—about 1,000 daily—to repopulate the colony. The much larger queen mates with the few hundred male drones while the female worker bees tend to the needs of the entire colony.

Queen Bee

A worker bee visits many flowers to collect nectar and pollen. The yellow dust catches on the bee's body, and she fills the pollen baskets on her hind legs with pollen. Once the honeybee returns to the hive, workers surround the bee to clean pollen from the hairs on her body. They empty the pollen baskets to be stored in the honeycomb cells.

The foraging bee returns to the hive with the collected nectar in her honey stomach, an organ for temporary nectar storage which adds important enzymes to the nectar. Upon arrival, the bee **regurgitates** the nectar to another bee in the hive. The receiving bee repeatedly **regurgitates** small amounts of the nectar, which allows it to air dry. When it is just right, she deposits it into a cell as honey. The constant fanning of the bees' wings further reduces the moisture content of the honey. When the process is complete, a worker bee caps the cell with wax.

We use honey as a sweetener and for its natural benefits. Honey soothes sore throats and suppresses coughs. Honey attracts and retains moisture, making it an ideal ingredient in cleansers, lotions, and hair products.

Honey never spoils because germs and bacteria cannot grow in honey. Even if crystals form, the honey is still edible.

Honeybees make a thick, white, nutritious substance called royal jelly. The worker bees feed larvae this bee milk for the first three days of life. A queen bee "in training" is fed royal jelly throughout her entire larval stage, which lasts about ten days. Some people use royal jelly for its medicinal properties.

Honeybees **secrete** wax flakes from the underside of their abdomen to mold into honeycomb and to cap cells for honey storage. These hexagonal cells provide a place for the queen to lay eggs and for the larvae and pupa to mature. Honey and pollen are also stored in the wax honeycomb cells.

Beekeepers obtain beeswax after removing honey the bees do not need to live through the winter. After the honey is removed from the beeswax, beekeepers melt and strain the wax before pouring it into a mold. Beeswax is used for candles, crayons, cosmetics, and ointments. Waxes can also be used for car, furniture, and floor care.

Smooth as Silk: Silkworm

Many insects and spiders produce silk thread, but only the silk from the silkworm's cocoon is used to manufacture luxurious silk fabric. The threads from the caterpillar of the silk moth are exceptionally long, strong, and elastic, making it highly desirable.

Silk dates back more than 5,000 years to the beginning of Chinese civilization. The Chinese people controlled silk production and guarded the industry's secrets. China held the monopoly in the silk industry for thousands of years until the Persians and Byzantines learned how to breed silkworms. Gradually, sericulture, or silk farming, spread through East Asia and Europe. The use of silk became popular throughout the world.

A single silk moth lays up to 500 tiny, yellow eggs. A group of 40,000 eggs weigh just one ounce (28 grams). That's as much as an individual box of raisins!

As a caterpillar, a silkworm feeds exclusively on the leaves of a mulberry tree. After its fourth and final **molt**, the caterpillar produces a continuous silk thread from its **salivary glands**. It spends about two days weaving the silk into a protective cocoon for its final stage of **metamorphosis**.

Sericulturists harvest the cocoons before the emergence of the adult silk moth. They place the cocoons in boiling water. This kills the pupa and allows the thread to unwind more easily.

A single silkworm cocoon has up to 3,000 feet (914 meters) of continuous silk filament. This fine silk thread is much finer than a strand of human hair. Several silk threads are woven together to produce a thicker, more usable thread, which is later woven into fabric and yarn. Silk cloth is strong and durable with a smooth texture.

The silk moth does not fly or even eat. Its only purpose is to reproduce and lay eggs. The silk moth only lives for about three days as an adult.

23

As **domestic** insects, silk moths fully rely upon humans for survival and reproduction. Even with **synthetic** fabrics such as nylon, silk remains an important product. Comfortable and lightweight, silk fabric is ideal for undergarments, shirts, dresses, ties, scarves, and other clothing. The fabric's durability provides enough strength for furniture upholstery and fine tapestries.

Hard as Nails: Lac Scale Insects

Substances used in the protective finishes of shellacs, called resins, have long been important as decorative materials. Around 1200 BCE, the people of India began to use resins made from the native lac scale insect. By the seventeenth century, lac resins became important in Europe. Later, resin use from lac insects spread to most of the industrialized world.

Lac females live on and infest branches of fig and other trees. They deposit lac liquid from their abdomens onto young tree branches. The lac hardens as it dries. To harvest the lac, the branches are removed from the tree. The harvesters scrape the hardened lac from branches. They grind the lac, then filter and refine it. As melted lac cools and hardens, it is stretched paper-thin and flaked. A pound of lac flakes, used for resins and shellac, requires up to 90,000 lac insects.

Only five percent of lac insects are male. They die after fertilizing multiple female lac insects.

Shellac, a popular liquid resin product, provides a clear, hard, protective coating to surfaces like wood and metal. It can be carved with ornamental designs.

Lac also provides a stiffening agent for products such as hats and shoes. It seals the wooden planks of boats watertight. It provides shine for the finish of artificial fruit, playing cards, and nail polish.

Lac products are also used in foods. Shellac is a primary ingredient in many edible **glazes**. As a coating on pills, it hides odors and makes medication easier to swallow. Shellac is also found in shiny candy coatings.

LOOK FOR IT!

As a food ingredient, lac is often listed as confectioner's glaze or resinous glaze.

Glossary

colony (KAH-luh-nee): a large group of animals that live together

domestic (duh-MES-tik): animals that have been tamed

glazes (GLAYZ-ez): liquids used to form coatings on food

metamorphosis (met-uh-MOR-fuh-seez): a series of changes some animals, such as caterpillars, go through as they develop into adults

molt (MOHLT): to lose old fur, feathers, or skin so that new ones can grow

regurgitates (ri-GUR-ji-tates): to bring food that has been swallowed back up to your mouth

salivary glands (SAL-uh-ver-ee GLANDS): small organs that produce saliva in the mouth

secrete (si-KREET): to produce and release a liquid

synthetic (sin-THET-ik): manufactured or artificial rather than found in nature

textiles (TEK-stiles): woven or knitted fabric or cloth

Index

Show What You Know

1. What purpose does carminic acid serve the cochineal scale insect?

2. Describe how a honeybee makes honey.

3. With synthetic materials available, why do people still use silk?

4. Name three ways lac resins are used.

5. Products of four insects were described in this book. Which insect's body is part of the product people use?

Websites to Visit

http://animals.nationalgeographic.com/animals/bugs

www.askentomologists.com

www.insects.org

About The Author

Annette Whipple learned to love science and nature during her years as an environmental educator and classroom teacher. She lives with her husband and three children in southeastern Pennsylvania where she enjoys baking, writing, and reading. Annette provides educational workshops for children focusing on science and pioneer life. Learn more about her at www.AnnetteWhipple.com.

www.rourkeeducationalmedia.com

PHOTO CREDITS: Cover: © SofiaWorld, Shaiith; Page 1: © Javy Najera Photography; Page 3: © Valentina Proskvrina; Page 4: © Frank Vincentz; Page 5: © sharptoyou; Page 6: © Spumador, Dr. Morley Read; Page 7: © Vahe Martirosyan, Whitney Cranshaw - Colorado State University - Bugwood.org; Page 8: © Eva Lepiz; Page 9: © Meaofoto, Everything, Natapol Chananuwong, Ditty-about-summer; Page 10: © Skynavin, Tyler Olson; Page 11: © Lehrer; Page 12: © Mirek Kijewski; Page 13: © Lehrer; Page 14: © ADA-photo, id-art; Page 15: © Lehrer; Page 16: © Darios; Page 17: © Marc Bruxelle; Page 18: © bunyarit; Page 19: © Sardius; Page 20: © Fuyu liv, Patricia Chumillas; Page 21: © Subin Pumsom; Page 22: © Sarayut Hyongsit; Page 23: © Yaipearn, Patricia Chumillas; Page 24: © Piyavachar Nacchanandana; Page 25: © Sergey Novikov; Page 26–27: © Jeffrey W. Lotz - Florida Department of Agriculture - Bugwood.org; Page 28: © blacksheep; Page 29: © Irina Kozorog Korta

Edited by: Keli Sipperley
Cover and Interior design by: Tara Raymo www.creativelytara.com

Library of Congress PCN Data

Insects as Producers / Annette Whipple
(Insects As …)
ISBN (hard cover)(alk. paper) 978-1-68191-697-2
ISBN (soft cover) 978-1-68191-798-6
ISBN (e-Book) 978-1-68191-896-9
Library of Congress Control Number: 2016932574

Printed in the United States of America, North Mankato, Minnesota

Also Available as:

3 1333 04634 6944